CARMEL CLAY PUBLIC LIBRARY

S0-BRW-528

TAKING A STAND

THE STANDING ROCK SIOUX
CHALLENGE THE DAKOTA ACCESS PIPELINE

by Clara MacCarald

FOCUS READERS

www.focusreaders.com

Copyright © 2019 by Focus Readers, Lake Elmo, MN 55042. All rights reserved. No part of this book may be reproduced or utilized in any form or by any means without written permission from the publisher.

Focus Readers is distributed by North Star Editions:
sales@northstareditions.com | 888-417-0195

Produced for Focus Readers by Red Line Editorial.

Content Consultant: Bruce E. Johansen, Professor of Communication and Native American Studies, University of Nebraska at Omaha

Photographs ©: Michael Nigro/Pacific Press/Sipa USA/AP Images, cover, 1, 36–37; David Goldman/AP Images, 4–5, 20–21, 22, 33; Nati Harnik/AP Images, 6; LM Otero/AP Images, 8–9; Red Line Editorial, 10; Albin Lohr-Jones/Pacific Press/Newscom, 13; Shutterstock Images, 14–15, 16, 18, 28–29, 31, 39; Mike McCleary/The Bismarck Tribune/AP Images, 25, 40; Dan Kraker/Minnesota Public Radio/AP Images, 27; Kevin Cederstrom/AP Images, 35; Evan Frost/Minnesota Public Radio/AP Images, 42–43; Scott Stockdill/North Dakota Department of Health/AP Images, 44

Library of Congress Cataloging-in-Publication Data
Names: MacCarald, Clara, 1979- author.
Title: The Standing Rock Sioux challenge the Dakota Access Pipeline / by
   Clara MacCarald.
Description: Lake Elmo, MN : Focus Readers, [2019] | Series: Taking a stand |
   Audience: Grades 7-8. | Includes bibliographical references and index. |
   Identifiers: LCCN 2018028295 (print) | LCCN 2018029265 (ebook) | ISBN
   9781641855334 (PDF) | ISBN 9781641854757 (ebook) | ISBN 9781641853590
   (hardcover : alk. paper) | ISBN 9781641854177 (pbk. : alk. paper)
Subjects: LCSH: Indians of North America--Political activity--Standing Rock
   Indian Reservation (N.D. and S.D.)--Juvenile literature. | Indians of
   North America--Standing Rock Indian Reservation (N.D. and
   S.D.)--Government relations--Juvenile literature. | Environmental
   justice--Standing Rock Indian Reservation (N.D. and S.D.)--Juvenile
   literature. | Petroleum pipelines--Standing Rock Indian Reservation (N.D.
   and S.D.)--Juvenile literature. | Standing Rock Sioux Tribe of North &
   South Dakota--Juvenile literature.
Classification: LCC E99.D1 (ebook) | LCC E99.D1 M197 2019 (print) | DDC
   978.4/88--dc23
LC record available at https://lccn.loc.gov/2018028295

Printed in the United States of America
Mankato, MN
October, 2018

ABOUT THE AUTHOR

Clara MacCarald is a freelance writer with a master's degree in biology. She lives with her family in an off-grid house nestled in the forests of central New York. When not parenting her daughter, she spends her time writing nonfiction books for kids.

TABLE OF CONTENTS

CHAPTER 1

INDIGENOUS PEOPLES' DAY

On October 10, 2016, a car drove through the Oceti Sakowin camp. Oceti Sakowin, or the Seven Council Fires, refers to the seven bands of the Sioux Nation. The camp was in North Dakota near the Standing Rock Sioux **Reservation**.

A drumbeat called for people to awaken. It was **Indigenous** Peoples' Day. Many people in the camp belonged to the Sioux Nation or other indigenous groups from across the Americas.

An upside-down flag waves above the Oceti Sakowin camp. It serves as a symbol of distress.

According to the company building it, the Dakota Access Pipeline created 12,000 temporary construction jobs.

They had come to support the Standing Rock Sioux Tribe. After praying and singing, people in the camp drove over dirt roads to a nearby construction site. Giant pieces of pipe lay on bare ground. Workers were constructing a pipeline that would stretch 1,200 miles (1,900 km) from North Dakota to Illinois.

The construction was set to go through land that was **sacred** to the Standing Rock Sioux.

The pipe would eventually go under the Missouri River. But if the pipe leaked, it would pollute the drinking water for the Standing Rock Reservation. People from the camp planned to stop progress on the pipeline. Some had already chained themselves to construction equipment early that morning. That way, workers wouldn't be able to build the pipeline.

The newcomers set up and decorated a tipi. They prayed and danced. But before long, the police began to arrive. They arrested people who didn't move back to the road. The protesters returned to the camp, but they weren't going home. They were taking a stand.

THINK ABOUT IT ◄

Would you risk arrest to support a cause you believed in? Why or why not?

CHAPTER 2

THE BLACK SNAKE

In April 2016, the Army Corps of Engineers was busy studying a proposal. A company called Energy Transfer Partners was building the Dakota Access Pipeline (DAPL). This massive pipeline would take oil from wells in North Dakota and carry it to Illinois to be purified. When finished, the pipeline would cross four states. It would carry at least 470,000 barrels (75,000 cubic meters) of oil per day.

A child protests the Dakota Access Pipeline, also known as the black snake.

The pipeline needed to cross public land controlled by the Corps. This land was near the Standing Rock Reservation. In 1851, the US government signed a treaty recognizing that the land belonged to the Standing Rock Sioux Tribe. The tribe believes it still owns this land, since it never legally gave up the area.

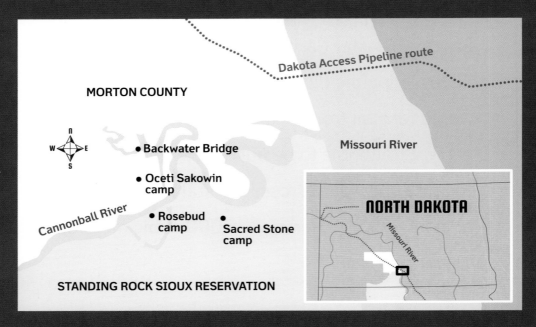

STANDING ROCK VS. THE PIPELINE

Dakota Access Pipeline route

MORTON COUNTY

Missouri River

N
W E
S

• Backwater Bridge

• Oceti Sakowin camp

Cannonball River

• Rosebud camp

• Sacred Stone camp

NORTH DAKOTA

Missouri River

STANDING ROCK SIOUX RESERVATION

The land in question has sites of cultural importance to the Standing Rock Sioux. These sites include a sacred burial ground and groups of stones with historical significance. The Corps noted five cultural sites on the land and more than 30 others that were thought to be nearby. Construction could disturb or destroy these sites.

The tribe worried that the government wouldn't listen to its concerns. While the Corps continued its study, a small group of American Indians rode through the reservation. The group included members of several indigenous nations. They set up camp near where the pipeline would cross. People lit sacred fires to bless the camp.

The group had come to protest the pipeline, which they called the black snake. Some of the Standing Rock Sioux belong to the Lakota nation. An old Lakota **prophecy** warned them of a snake.

One day, a black snake would slither across the land. It would destroy land and poison water, just as people feared the pipeline would do.

The Standing Rock Sioux continued to make their case to the US government. On July 15, American Indian youth began a relay run from North Dakota to Washington, DC. They covered nearly 2,000 miles (3,219 km) over 25 days. At the end, they delivered more than 160,000 signatures against the pipeline. But their efforts failed. On July 25, 2016, the Corps approved the request for the pipeline to cross the Missouri River near Standing Rock.

The Standing Rock Sioux **sued** the Corps on August 4. But the pipeline was going ahead anyway. As construction crews neared the river, the tribe complained that they were destroying traditional sites.

Native youth protest in New York City after finishing their relay race to Washington, DC.

On August 10, construction workers arrived for the day. But this time, they were met by protesters. The number of protesters grew over the next few days. At one point, protesters broke through fences to reach the construction site. There, private security guards waited with dogs. The two groups clashed, and the dogs bit some of the protesters. The fight was heating up.

CHAPTER 3

WATER PROTECTORS

Thousands of people set up tipis, tents, and campers on several sites near the Missouri River. They called themselves water protectors.

The water protectors had come to stand up for indigenous rights. For many indigenous groups, Standing Rock was just the latest battle in the fight for their land and people. The US government has recognized the **sovereignty** of American Indian tribes for more than 150 years.

A signpost at the Oceti Sakowin camp points toward places represented by water protectors.

The tribes have the right to govern their own lands and people. But the US government has broken many of its treaties and refused to protect American Indians from settlers looking for land.

The US government has also failed to protect tribes from pollution. Industries have polluted reservations through mining operations. In 2005, the Navajo Nation banned mining of nuclear material. The ban came after cancers related to mining had killed hundreds of people.

More than 200 American Indian tribes in North America declared their support for the Standing

Rock Sioux. Indigenous people from around the world came to join the movement. Their tribal flags waved above the camp. Some people had helped fight pipeline construction in the past.

The last time the seven bands of the Sioux people came together was in 1876. The Sioux had joined Cheyenne and Arapaho tribes to protect their land from settlers. When US soldiers attacked, the American Indians defeated them at the Battle of Little Bighorn. They forced the US government to consider their rights to the land. The water protectors hoped they, too, could convince the US government to listen.

THINK ABOUT IT ◁

Many tribes that joined the water protectors were not affected by the pipeline. Why do you think they supported the Standing Rock Sioux?

Water protectors had other concerns, too. Many wanted to keep fossil fuels in the ground. Fossil fuels, such as oil, form underground over millions of years. When taken out of the ground, fossil fuels can be burned to produce power. But burning fossil fuels releases greenhouse gases into Earth's atmosphere. These gases keep heat from escaping

GLOBAL WARMING

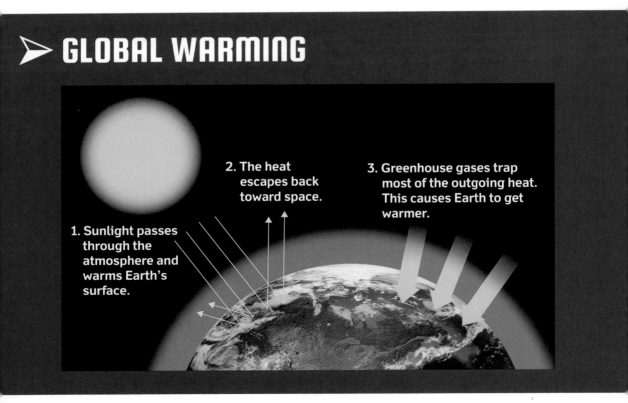

1. Sunlight passes through the atmosphere and warms Earth's surface.

2. The heat escapes back toward space.

3. Greenhouse gases trap most of the outgoing heat. This causes Earth to get warmer.

into space. Increased levels of greenhouse gases are slowly warming the planet, which leads to many environmental problems. This process is known as global warming.

People who are concerned about global warming often oppose pipelines. Pipelines make it cheaper for companies to ship oil. For this reason, some people think pipelines encourage companies to produce oil more quickly. But supporters of pipelines argue that oil would still be produced without pipelines. It would have to be shipped by train, which creates more greenhouse gases.

Non-indigenous people also arrived to support the Standing Rock Sioux. They included **activists**, lawyers, politicians, and others. The group Black Lives Matter sent people to visit the camps. They connected the American Indians' fight for water with black communities' fight against pollution.

CHAPTER 4

LIFE IN THE CAMPS

The water protectors' camps sprawled across private and federal land. Some people drove to reach the camps. Others traveled on the water they were protecting. Members of tribes in the Pacific West, such as the Quinault Indian Nation, traveled to Bismarck, North Dakota, and canoed down the Missouri River. The camps seemed like small towns with families, friends, and strangers all living together.

Members of the Colville Confederated Tribes arrive by canoe at the Oceti Sakowin camp.

A A member of the Colville Nez Perce tribe drums with water protectors.

Like any town, the camps needed certain things to function. People at the camps ran large kitchens that fed several hundred people each day. They split wood for campfires and hauled water. For fun, people enjoyed spending time with their friends. They could ride horses and swim in nearby waterways. Children attended classes at the camps when school was in session.

A large fire pit in the main camp drew people together for prayer, drumming, and meetings. The leaders among the water protectors wanted people in the camps to get along. They asked people not to bring alcohol or drugs. They also requested that non-indigenous people respect the traditions of indigenous people. This could mean not wearing certain traditional clothing or attending certain ceremonies.

Some people took on special roles to help the camps run smoothly. Young men on horseback ran errands and delivered messages. They called themselves spirit riders. Doctors and traditional healers also offered their services. People who had legal questions could even visit a tent full of lawyers.

Although people often enjoyed living together in the camps, they had come to protect the water.

A few people controlled **drones** to monitor construction of the pipeline. Others scouted on horseback. People demonstrated nearly every day. They marched on the road leading to the construction site. Some carried tribal flags or wore traditional clothing from their indigenous group. Sometimes, the water protectors blocked trucks and equipment. They often prayed and performed ceremonies opposing the pipeline.

The demonstrations brought the water protectors into conflict with police and private security forces. These forces kept a close eye on the camps. They flew aircraft and drones overhead. Police accused water protectors of throwing small bombs and starting fires. They said people were rioting and trespassing. The water protectors countered that the police used too much force.

Water protectors clashed with officers in the Cantapeta Creek near the Oceti Sakowin camp.

Police at the camps had tanks and **riot gear**. They used pepper spray, water cannons, and rubber bullets against the water protectors. They also arrested and charged hundreds of people with crimes. Actor Shailene Woodley and Green Party presidential candidate Jill Stein were among the people arrested. The police jailed water protectors in cages and wrote numbers on their arms to identify them. In response, a group from the **United Nations** investigated the police for human rights abuse.

WINONA LADUKE

Winona LaDuke is an Anishinaabe activist from the White Earth Reservation in Minnesota. In September 2016, LaDuke spoke to a journalist while visiting the Standing Rock camps. In LaDuke's opinion, the people on the reservation didn't need a pipeline. They needed better houses, better highways, and better sources of energy. "They're looking at a 3.9-billion-dollar pipeline that will not help them," said LaDuke. "It will only help oil companies. And so that's why we're here."

LaDuke had previously helped protest a pipeline in Minnesota. "We attended every hearing. . . . We rode our horses against the current of the oil. We had ceremonies. And they cancelled the pipeline." LaDuke went on to explain the importance of protesting pipelines. "This matters because it's time to move on from fossil fuels."

△ Winona LaDuke (center) and other activists protest a pipeline that would cross Minnesota.

DAPL protests were especially important for the Standing Rock Sioux, who had already lost so much. "In my community, we have rice. We still have our wild rice," LaDuke said. But the Standing Rock Sioux had lost ways to make a living off their land. White settlers had wiped out their buffalo population. "This is their stand," LaDuke said of the Standing Rock Sioux. "They've got a chance to not have one more bad thing happen to them."

Amy Goodman. "Native American Activist Winona LaDuke at Standing Rock: It's Time to Move On from Fossil Fuels." *Democracy Now!* Democracy Now!, 12 Sept. 2016. Web. 6 June 2018.

CHAPTER 5

WINTER CLOSES IN

On September 8, 2016, North Dakota governor Jack Dalrymple called on the National Guard to oppose the water protectors. On September 9, a judge ruled that the Corps had consulted with the Standing Rock Sioux long enough. He decided that work on the pipeline should continue. But the US government disagreed. Officials thought the Corps should continue discussions with the tribe.

When winter came, water protectors stayed warm by building fires in tipis.

The government asked Energy Transfer Partners to pause construction. During a White House Tribal Nations Conference, US president Barack Obama told American Indian leaders that Standing Rock was being heard. But despite the government's request, the company started work again in October.

Late fall brought heavy snow and freezing temperatures. Police continued to spray water cannons, which can be deadly in such conditions. Some water protectors were taken to the hospital for **hypothermia**. Others were treated for injuries from rubber bullets. In November, the United Nations condemned the police's actions.

In late November, the Corps told water protectors in the main camp to leave federal land. Soon after, Dalrymple ordered the area to be evacuated. State officials closed a bridge where

SPEED LIMIT 45

NEXT 1 MILES

In response to protests, state officials closed off Backwater Bridge.

police and water protectors had clashed. This bridge connected the Standing Rock Reservation with outside cities. With the bridge closed, people in the camps struggled to get supplies.

Despite these challenges, the water protectors refused to move. Most lived without electricity. They even marched in blizzards. The water protectors also worked to share their message with the public. They spoke to journalists and posted on social media.

Some members of the public donated supplies to the camps. People outside the camps helped in other ways, too. At one point, water protectors feared the police could use social media data to identify them. In response, more than one million people falsely posted on Facebook that they were at the camps. They wanted to confuse the police.

Other people supported the pipeline. Energy Transfer Partners argued that the pipeline was unlikely to pollute the Missouri River. The company also said the pipeline would help the United States produce more of its own fossil fuels. That way, it could import less from other nations.

On December 4, the Standing Rock Sioux had a victory. The Corps announced that the pipeline would not be allowed to pass near Standing Rock. It had made the decision after receiving pressure from the Obama administration. Construction

 Water protectors celebrate the December 4, 2016, decision to halt pipeline construction.

halted. The Corps began an environmental review of other routes. They would not allow construction to continue until the review was complete.

Many water protectors felt they had won. People celebrated into the night under the flash of fireworks. Dave Archambault II, the chairman of the Standing Rock Sioux Tribe, asked people to leave because of the danger posed by winter.

DAVE ARCHAMBAULT II

On October 24, 2016, Dave Archambault II sent a letter to US Attorney General Loretta Lynch. He wrote, "The Standing Rock Sioux Tribe has a strong interest in protecting our Treaty rights, our sacred sites, and our waters. . . . Thousands of people from around the country, and the world, have come to express their opposition to the pipeline in a peaceful way."

As chairman of the Standing Rock Sioux Tribe, Archambault was concerned about the safety of the water protectors. He thought the police's responses were unjust. The police had allowed private security guards to attack people with dogs and pepper spray. Archambault called on Lynch to investigate these behaviors.

"This country has a long and sad history of using military force against indigenous people—including the Sioux Nation," he wrote.

▲ Dave Archambault II was chairman of the Standing Rock Sioux Tribe from 2013 to 2017.

Archambault compared the police's tactics with those used during the civil rights movement of the 1950s and 1960s. He wrote that the government often investigates only after something terrible happens. "I hope and pray that you will see the wisdom of acting now in an effort to prevent such a tragedy here."

Dave Archambault II. "Dave Archambault II to Loretta Lynch, 24 Oct. 2016." Contributed by Rebecca Hersher, National Public Radio. Web. 6 June 2018.

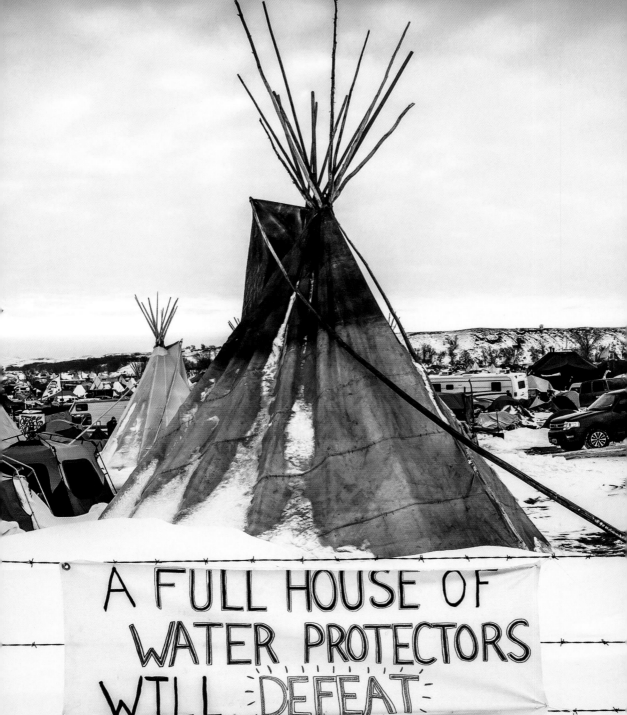

CHAPTER 6

END OF THE CAMPS

Despite the water protectors' victory, the fight wasn't over. In January 2017, Donald Trump became president of the United States. During his campaign, Trump had promised to support fossil fuels. The head of Energy Transfer Partners had donated $100,000 to Trump's campaign. In the past, Trump had invested money in companies linked to the pipeline. However, a spokesperson claimed he no longer had those investments.

Water protectors posted signs in protest of Donald Trump.

Water protectors feared Trump would reverse the Corps's decision to halt construction.

On January 24, the water protectors' worst fears came true. Trump issued an executive order. The order told the Corps to quickly approve the permit for the pipeline to cross the Missouri River near Standing Rock. It also asked the Corps to withdraw its environmental review, even though the review wasn't finished. Archambault pleaded with Trump to change his mind.

Trump's orders were met within two weeks. The Corps approved the permit for the pipeline to go under the Missouri River. Only 1.5 miles (2.4 km) of work remained. Construction started up again.

State officials ordered the main camp to be evacuated by February 22. They said it was dangerous for water protectors to stay. Spring rains would soon flood the area. But the officials

Protesters around the country rallied against Trump's executive order.

had another reason for evacuating the camp. They didn't want water protectors to disrupt construction. Soon, water protectors began to leave the camp. They gathered what they could. Some set fire to tents and other structures they had to leave behind. Others remained at the camp. They were determined to resist the pipeline as long as possible.

Law enforcement enters the Oceti Sakowin camp to begin arrests.

Police officers and National Guard soldiers surrounded the camp. On February 23, they marched inside. They wore riot gear and carried rifles. The officers arrested everyone who remained in the camp. Afterward, they used heavy equipment to tear down the structures left behind.

The Standing Rock Sioux did not give up in court. But without water protectors at the camp, work on the pipeline moved quickly. In April 2017, before it was even finished, the pipeline leaked 84 gallons (318 L) of oil in South Dakota. Archambault pointed to the leak as evidence of the pipeline's danger. But Energy Transfer Partners played down the leak. They said it was small and easily fixed.

By June, oil began flowing. On June 14, the tribe received another small victory. A judge ruled that the Corps's original survey wasn't good enough. According to a treaty, the Standing Rock Sioux have hunting and fishing rights. But the Corps hadn't fully considered how a spill might affect game animals and fish. The judge ordered the Corps to do more studies, but he didn't stop the pipeline from carrying oil.

CHAPTER 7

THE SPIRIT OF STANDING ROCK

Despite the water protectors' fight, DAPL became a fully functioning pipeline. The Standing Rock Sioux worried the oil would pollute their water. The water protectors were also still facing effects of their demonstrations. Some faced charges in court from their time at the camps. Others had lasting injuries.

Companies that build pipelines insist that spills are unlikely. However, large spills happen.

Today, cattle graze on the land of the now-empty Oceti Sakowin camp.

⬧ In December 2016, the Belle Fourche Pipeline had one of the largest spills in North Dakota history.

In December 2016, a pipeline in North Dakota leaked 530,000 gallons (2,006,000 L) of oil. The spill occurred while water protectors were protesting DAPL. And in November 2017, the Keystone Pipeline in South Dakota leaked 210,000 gallons (795,000 L) of oil.

The Standing Rock Sioux didn't give up. The water protectors' protests had succeeded in halting construction at times. Energy Transfer Partners lost $100 million because of halted construction. On top of that, the company lost another $3 million when a bank took back its investment. As of 2018, the Standing Rock Sioux and three other tribes continued to fight the pipeline in court.

Many water protectors have moved on to other battles. They continue to fight for indigenous rights and environmental justice. Some of these activists are young people who lived in the camps. Activists have also fought to stop pipelines planned for states such as Minnesota, Louisiana, and Texas. Although the camps have closed, the spirit of Standing Rock lives on.

THINK ABOUT IT ◄

Do you think the DAPL protests were worth it, even though the water protectors lost? Why or why not?

FOCUS ON
THE STANDING ROCK SIOUX

Write your answers on a separate piece of paper.

1. Write a sentence describing the water protectors' reasons for protesting the Dakota Access Pipeline.

2. Do you think the Dakota Access Pipeline should have been built? Why or why not?

3. Who called on the National Guard to oppose the water protectors?
- **A.** North Dakota governor Jack Dalrymple
- **B.** US president Donald Trump
- **C.** US president Barack Obama

4. What would have happened if Donald Trump had not signed the executive order about Standing Rock?
- **A.** Energy Transfer Partners would have started building the rest of the pipeline.
- **B.** Construction would have remained halted until the Corps finished its study.
- **C.** Oil would have started flowing through the pipeline under the Missouri River.

Answer key on page 48.

GLOSSARY

activists
People who take action to make social or political changes.

drones
Aircraft or ships that are controlled remotely or operate on their own.

hypothermia
The loss of body heat to a level much lower than normal.

indigenous
Native to a region, or belonging to ancestors who did not immigrate to the region.

prophecy
A prediction of something that will happen in the future.

reservation
An area of land set aside for American Indian people.

riot gear
Protective clothing and equipment that police wear when they expect to deal with violent crowds.

sacred
Having spiritual or religious meaning.

sovereignty
The power to make rules and decisions without being controlled by another country.

sued
Took legal action against a person or institution.

United Nations
A worldwide organization that promotes international cooperation.

TO LEARN MORE

BOOKS

Edwards, Sue Bradford. *The Dakota Access Pipeline.*
 Minneapolis: Abdo Publishing, 2018.
Hand, Carol. *Climate Change: Our Warming Earth.*
 Minneapolis: Abdo Publishing, 2015.
Lawton, Cassie M. *The People and Culture of the Sioux.*
 New York: Cavendish Square, 2017.

NOTE TO EDUCATORS

Visit **www.focusreaders.com** to find lesson plans, activities, links, and other resources related to this title.

INDEX

Answer Key: **1.** Answers will vary; **2.** Answers will vary; **3.** A; **4.** B